1 Peter

Confidence in a Complex World

A six-session Bible study for individuals and small groups

By Joe Warton

licc.

*But you are a chosen people,
a royal priesthood, a holy nation,
a people belonging to God,
that you may declare the praises
of him who called you into his
wonderful light.*

1 Peter 2:9

INTER-VARSITY PRESS
36 Causton Street, London SW1P 4ST, England
Email: ivp@ivpbooks.com
Website: www.ivpbooks.com

First published 2019

British Library Cataloguing-in-Publication Data
A catalogue record for this book is available from the British Library

ISBN: 978–1–78974–086–8
eBook ISBN: 978–1–78974–087–5

Typeset in Great Britain by Sublime
Print and production managed in Great Britain by Jellyfish Print Solutions

Inter-Varsity Press publishes Christian books that are true to the
Bible and that communicate the gospel, develop discipleship
and strengthen the church for its mission in the world.

IVP originated within the Inter-Varsity Fellowship, now the
Universities and Colleges Christian Fellowship, a student movement
connecting Christian Unions in universities and colleges throughout
Great Britain, and a member movement of the International
Fellowship of Evangelical Students. Website: www.uccf.org.uk.
That historic association is maintained, and all senior IVP staff
and committee members subscribe to the UCCF Basis of Faith.

Contents

The Gateway Seven

Exodus Law

Ezekiel Prophecy

Mark Gospel

1 Peter Letters

Proverbs Wisdom

Revelation Apocalyptic

Ruth Narrative

The Gateway Seven Bible Study Series

We don't approach a novel in the same way we tackle a legal document. We don't read poetry in the same way we might read a letter from a friend. So, we don't read the 66 books of the Bible as if they were all the same kind of writing. Story, song, law, letter, and more, all make up the rich repository of writing that together is God's word to us.

For *The Gateway Seven* series we've selected seven books of the Bible that each represent a different kind of writing. The mini-features sprinkled through the studies, together with the questions suggested for discussion, invite you to explore each book afresh in a way that's sensitive to its genre as well as to the concerns of the book itself.

Each study engages with a different kind of writing. However, each one in the series has been crafted with the same central desire: to offer a gateway to a deeper love of God's word and richer insights into its extraordinary implications for all of life, Monday through Sunday.

'May your kingdom come – on earth as in heaven', Jesus taught us to pray. May your kingdom come in our homes and places of work and service. May your kingdom come at the school gate as well as in the sanctuary. May your kingdom come in the hydrotherapy pool, in the council chamber, on the estate, around the Board table. May your kingdom come as we learn to live our everyday lives as beloved sons and daughters, wondrously wrapped up in our Father's 'family business'.

Our prayer is that these seven distinctive books of the Bible will be a gateway for you to a richer, deeper, transforming life with God wherever you are – seven days a week.

Tracy Cotterell

The Gateway Seven Series Editor
Managing Director - Mission, LICC

Making the Most of 1 Peter

Introduction to 1 Peter
Confidence in a Complex World

'Peter, an apostle of Jesus Christ, To God's elect, exiles, scattered throughout the provinces of Pontus, Galatia, Cappadocia, Asia and Bithynia, who have been chosen according to the foreknowledge of God the Father, through the sanctifying work of the Spirit, to be obedient to Jesus Christ and sprinkled with his blood: Grace and peace be yours in abundance.' 1 Peter 1:1-2

When Peter writes to small groups of Christians scattered across the country we now call Turkey, he's longing for them to live well as the people of God in a complex world. So, he starts by using two pivotal words to describe them and then he reminds them of a stunning truth.

Firstly, they're God's elect. From Genesis 12 onwards, it's clear that God's purpose was that Abraham and all his descendants would be blessed and would be a blessing to the world around. Writing to these early Christians, most of whom would not have been Jews by birth, Peter draws them into the ongoing story of God's intention for the world by using the language of calling – 'chosen', 'elect'.

Secondly, they're exiles. Here, Peter recalls the great disaster of the Old Testament – when Israel lost their land. At first, their only hope was in a quick return, but the prophets told them that most of that first generation of exiles would not return, though they could remain distinct and be a blessing where they were (Jeremiah 29).

Finally, Peter reminds them of the wondrous truth that God – Father, Son and Spirit – is at work in them. They are known – the Father's foreknowledge; they have been set apart – the Spirit's sanctifying work; they can be confident of their relationship with God through the Son – the sprinkling of blood is a sign of being included in his covenant. And so, they are called to be obedient to Jesus Christ in a complex world and know grace and peace in abundance.

As in Peter's day, we don't spend all our time with fellow Christians. We're scattered, often the only followers of Jesus on our street, at work, or even at home. These are our frontlines where, in our times, we are called to be distinctive and to make a difference for Christ. When we gather as worshippers, we remind ourselves that we believe a very particular story about the world. We believe it's God's – he created it. We believe it's broken – because of sin. We believe that Jesus' death makes new life possible. We believe that one day everything will be transformed. We live as people with a distinct story in a culture that may not believe any of that.

This study is a guide through Peter's letter written to people whose context he understood well and with which we can resonate today. Through his encouragement, challenge, insight, and knowledge of God – expressed first to them – we too will gain confidence to live well for Christ in our complex world, on our everyday frontlines.

An excellent 8-minute animated overview of the book of 1 Peter has been produced by **The Bible Project** at jointhebibleproject.com or search YouTube for: 'Read Scripture: 1 Peter'

Studying 1 Peter

This Bible study is designed to cover the whole of the letter in six sessions:

Session 1 | Confident in the Gospel (1 Peter 1:1–2:3)

Session 2 | Confident in Identity (1 Peter 2:4–10)

Session 3 | Confident in the World (1 Peter 2:11–25)

Session 4 | Confident in Relationships (1 Peter 3:1–12)

Session 5 | Confident in Witness (1 Peter 3:13–4:6)

Session 6 | Confident in Community (1 Peter 4:7–5:14)

In some of the sessions, the discussion is focused around a main section of the passage. However, the session guide covers the rest of the text in other ways, usually in the 'Going Deeper' part of the study. Groups can discuss this together or people might like to look at it on their own through the week.

You can work through each session on your own, one-to-one, or in a small group.

If your church is covering 1 Peter in a sermon series, this study is an ideal way to deepen your understanding of the letter and explore its implications for Monday to Saturday life. Working through the sessions in a group also encourages each person to share insights and stories of how they have seen God at work in their own context.

Each group has its own way of doing things, so the session plan is a suggestion, not a rule.

Suggested session plan

---

1 Pray to open

2 Read the 'First Thoughts' section

3 Read the passage from 1 Peter

4 Work through the questions

The questions cover different areas – the session's main theme, what the Bible passage says and means, going deeper, and living out the passage. Many questions don't have 'right' or 'wrong' answers. It's important and helpful to hear insights from everyone in the group. Group leaders may want to pick out the most pertinent questions for their group to discuss.

5 Pray to close

Don't feel bound by these prayer prompts if your study has taken a different turn. Be flexible in responding to each other's needs.

Dotted throughout this guide are brief feature pieces on questions or issues related to the background and study of 1 Peter. Together with some real-life stories – lived examples of how God's word can be worked out in daily life – they offer insights

Participating in the study

Before each session, you might like to read the passage together with one of the features, and any explanation boxes or stories that accompany the session. After you meet, you might like to pursue some of the 'Going Deeper' questions on your own.

Before the first session

1 Peter is a short letter so take a moment to read it through in one go before the first session, perhaps just simply noting down the things that strike you.

Another way to experience the whole of 1 Peter

Join LICC's digital devotional journey.
This is a series of daily readings through 1 Peter delivered through email or the YouVersion Bible app. Sign up at **licc.org.uk/ourresources.**

My frontline

Before you start the study, reflect on your frontline using these questions. Your frontline is an everyday place where you live, work, study, or play and where you're likely to connect with people who aren't Christians.

Where is your frontline?

What's going on there?
Who's with you there?

What are you excited about or struggling with?

What opportunities or challenges are you facing?

Come back to this reflection throughout the sessions, praying and trusting that God will direct your ways through his word.

How should we read the New Testament letters?

Reading the letters of the New Testament isn't that much different from reading a letter (or email) you've received from someone you know. The only difference is, you don't know the people who received these letters, and you don't know the people who sent them.

OK, that's quite a difference. There's definitely some thinking we'll need to do, but it's not like we're starting from square one here – we're already familiar with letters as a type of writing, or genre. For example, we know they're not written into a vacuum, but into real flesh and blood situations. Learning about the recipients and what was going on in their lives and communities, and how the author addresses these, is massively rewarding. It allows us to open up the meaning of biblical letters with all the joy of a child unwrapping a chocolate egg.

When it comes to reading New Testament letters, the single most helpful word to keep in mind is 'context'. In fact, that's the case when we read any book of the Bible. Sometimes we think we need an expert to help us understand the context of the letter. Of course, scholars offer us the fruit of their research in many fine commentaries and these can greatly enrich our reading of the Bible. But don't underestimate how much you can discover yourself by asking the 'who, what, where, when, why' questions when reading a letter closely. You'll start to appreciate the author's motivation in writing the letter, how that related to their understanding of what was going on, and what needed to be said. There are tons of clues lying within the letters themselves.

When we talk about context, we are talking about answers to questions like: who was the letter written to, and what challenges were they facing? What were they hoping for, and what questions were they asking? It can also help to understand a bit of background, like how did their society work, what was valued, who did they believe God to be, why did they behave in a particular way? The more you get a feel for who the people were and what they faced, the more you begin to see how the author's words will have soothed, surprised, stung, or stimulated their readers (or hearers as they might first have been).

So, as we read through 1 Peter with an inquisitive eye, what do we discover about Peter and his audience? Before you read on, you might want to jot down what you notice when you read the letter through in one go, asking the questions in the box on the next page.

The typical format for ancient letter-writing was to start by clarifying who the letter was from and to, and open with a greeting (1 Peter 1:1-2). Peter is writing to Christians scattered across what is now modern-day Turkey, and there is no indication that Peter had ever met them personally. Many scholars think this was a kind of circular letter which would be read out in lots of gatherings through these regions. Peter wants them to be clear that he has authority as 'an apostle of Jesus Christ' (1:1) and he makes it clear that his intentions for them are very good (1:2). He refers to them as 'Dear friends' in 2:11 and 4:12, and identifies himself alongside the elders of the churches to whom he writes (5:1).

As for his predominantly Gentile audience, it's clear that they have experienced real conversion, evidenced by the fruit of transformation. At one time, they had 'lived in ignorance' (1:14) and had not been the people of God (2:10), living as pagans who indulged in drunkenness, sexual immorality, and idolatry (4:3). But now, they 'have been born again', 'obeying the truth', and demonstrating love for each other 'from the heart' (1:22-23).

We also get a glimpse into their day-to-day lives, reminding us that these were real people, not religious cardboard cutouts. They lived 'among the pagans' (2:12), not in Christian ghettos. Some of them were slaves (2:18), some had husbands who did not believe (3:1-2), and many of them faced pressure from their non-Christian associates to engage in practices that were less than edifying (4:3-4).

And this meant suffering. Suffering is mentioned in every chapter of Peter's letter (e.g. 1:6, 2:20, 3:14, 4:1, 5:9). Peter's focus on suffering suggests we can safely deduce it was an all-too-familiar experience for these early Christians.

So, whatever letter of the New Testament you are reading on your own, studying in a group, or listening to sermons on in church, you can discover much more of its context yourself through a careful reading. You may then want to check out what a commentary or Bible background book has to say, but it's always good to see what you can find out yourself first. It's also much more fun!

Always keep context in mind

Some helpful context questions to keep in the back of your mind when reading letters. There may not be answers to all of them.

Who?
Who wrote the letter and who were the recipients? What does the letter tell us about them and are they mentioned anywhere else in the Bible?

What?
What happens in the letter? What's said? It's helpful to get a sense of the main themes of the letter, as this will help make more sense of the details.

When?
Are there any clues in the letter about when it was written? Is there a particular reason the author has chosen to write to them at this time?

Where?
Where are the recipients living? How does this help us understand the letter better?

Why?
Why has the author written this letter at all? In the ancient world, writing was a costly and time-consuming activity. All of the New Testament letters were written with purpose – to teach, rebuke, encourage, persuade. What do you think the author was hoping would happen as a result of writing these things to these people?

Session 1

Confident in the Gospel

1 Peter 1:1–2:3

First Thoughts

In 1581 Galileo's father sent him off to Pisa to study medicine. It quickly became apparent that Galileo had a remarkable flair for mathematics. He switched tracks and went on to make extraordinary discoveries in the field of astronomy.

At the time, the majority opinion about our solar system was geocentric; that the sun and other planets revolved around the earth. Galileo, on the other hand, had read Copernicus's theory that the earth revolved around the sun. The more Galileo investigated, the more he was convinced this was the case. Unfortunately for him, these convictions got him in trouble. Considered a dangerous heretic, he lived out his final days under house arrest. But he did not waver. His confidence in those truths shaped his life in profound and costly ways.

The apostle Peter was writing to groups of Christians who lived in societies where the gospel was seen as utter nonsense, and dangerous utter nonsense at that. Their newfound faith came under pressure and their confidence in the gospel was tested. Why should they remain confident in the gospel when everyone else around them was so sure this confidence was misplaced?

Read – 1 Peter 1:1-12

¹ Peter, an apostle of Jesus Christ, To God's elect, exiles, scattered throughout the provinces of Pontus, Galatia, Cappadocia, Asia and Bithynia, ² who have been chosen according to the foreknowledge of God the Father, through the sanctifying work of the Spirit, to be obedient to Jesus Christ and sprinkled with his blood: Grace and peace be yours in abundance. ³ Praise be to the God and Father of our Lord Jesus Christ! In his great mercy he has given us new birth into a living hope through the resurrection of Jesus Christ from the dead, ⁴ and into an inheritance that can never perish, spoil or fade. This inheritance is kept in heaven for you, ⁵ who through faith are shielded by God's power until the coming of the salvation that is ready to be revealed in the last time. ⁶ In all this you greatly rejoice, though now for a little while you may have had to suffer grief in all kinds of trials. ⁷ These have come so that the proven genuineness of your faith – of greater worth than gold, which perishes even though refined by fire – may result in praise, glory and honour when Jesus Christ is revealed. ⁸ Though you have not seen him, you love him; and even though you do not see him now, you believe in him and are filled with an inexpressible and glorious joy, ⁹ for you are receiving the end result of your faith, the salvation of your souls. ¹⁰ Concerning this salvation, the prophets, who spoke of the grace that was to come to you, searched intently and with the greatest care, ¹¹ trying to find out the time and circumstances to which the Spirit of Christ in them was pointing when he predicted the sufferings of the Messiah and the glories that would follow. ¹² It was revealed to them that they were not serving themselves but you, when they spoke of the things that have now been told you by those who have preached the gospel to you by the Holy Spirit sent from heaven. Even angels long to look into these things.

Focus on the Theme

1. Have you ever been in a difficult or scary situation, yet remained confident?

Where do you think that confidence came from?

How did that confidence help you to do what you needed to do?

What Does the Bible Say?

Read the 'Introduction to 1 Peter' (page 10) before jumping into 1:3-12.

2. In 1:3-5, Peter provides a glorious 'gospel nugget': a condensed insight into the rich treasure that is the good news of Jesus Christ for us and the world. What do you notice about how this gospel is 'good news' for those who trust in it?

3. According to Peter, why can this gospel be trusted? (1:3-12). You might like to divide the verses up between you and then pool your insights.

4. We know that the people Peter wrote to suffered for their faith. What is surprising about the way they responded to suffering 'grief in all kinds of trials' (1:6)?

Why do you think they responded in this way?

5. In 1:10-12, Peter mentions the role played by the Holy Spirit in guiding the Old Testament prophets, as well as those who had preached the gospel to them. How does the Holy Spirit's involvement further strengthen their confidence?

Going Deeper

6. Think about what Peter saw and experienced throughout his lifetime. Why do you think he had so much confidence in the gospel? (You may find it helpful to skim John 20:1-7, John 20:19-20, Acts 1:4-11, Acts 3:3-8, and Acts 10.)

7. In your Bible, take a look at 1:13-2:3. The passage starts with 'Therefore' – what Peter is about to tell them is linked to what he has just said about the gospel. What kind of life does this gospel call for?

Living it Out

8. How have the circumstances of your life and the beliefs of others around you impacted your own confidence in the gospel?

9. Think about one person that you meet on your frontline who is not a Christian. As far as you know, what do they think about the Christian faith and about Jesus Christ?

10. Based on what you've looked at so far, in what ways, if any, has Peter helped to strengthen your confidence in the gospel?

What impact do you think a greater confidence in the gospel would make in your life?

Prayer Time

- Thank God for the goodness, truth, and power of the gospel.

- Ask God to strengthen your confidence in this and to help you bear the fruit you desire.

- Thinking about the non-Christians you meet, what might help them take a step closer to Jesus? Pray for this together.

Indicatives and imperatives

An indicative is a simple statement of fact or truth. For example, '[God] has given us new birth into a living hope' (1:3), 'you are a chosen people' (2:9), and 'Christ died for sins once for all' (3:18) are all indicatives – they tell us what is. An imperative, on the other hand, is a command, a call to action. 'Live such good lives among the pagans' (2:12), and 'Humble yourselves' (5:6) are examples of imperatives.

New Testament letter-writers often start their letters primarily in 'indicative mode'. In other words, they dwell on truths such as who God is and what he's done, and who we are. Later in the letter they move more into 'imperative mode'. In other words, the authors are saying to us: on the basis of these wonderful truths that we can be confident in, now let's live our lives in these ways.

Living in exile – then and now

It was a radical change for these early Christians: turning away from their old way of life and embracing Christ. Being drawn into the heart of God's community meant being pushed to the outside of their earthly communities.

In becoming the people of God (2:10), they turned towards Christ and away from other gods. Doing so had repercussions (4:3-4, 12-16). Now they were targets of malicious accusations, their names now the 'x' in the 'have you heard about x?' conversations between neighbours or fellow slaves. Households, fields, markets, and streets, which might once have felt like home, did so no longer. They had become outsiders.

Peter understood their situation, he knew how they felt. He had seen this elsewhere (5:9). He'd experienced rejection himself. Knowing how they felt, and knowing who they were in Christ, he wanted to help them make sense of what was going on and renew their imagination of what life could be like in this old-yet-new world.

They were 'foreigners and exiles' (2:11). The word he uses for 'foreigners' means someone who is not a citizen of the area they currently inhabit, and an 'exile' is someone who will not stay there indefinitely. Peter was very happy to apply Old Testament language to New Testament followers of Christ, whether Jew or Gentile. In referring to them as 'foreigners and exiles', he's doing it again.

When living among the Hittites, Abraham, the father of the Jewish nation, described himself as 'a foreigner and stranger' (Genesis 23:4). And between the times when Abraham and Jesus walked the earth, the Jewish nation walked from Jerusalem to Babylon as exiles, before walking back again.

When Abraham found himself in a foreign land (willingly), and when the Jewish people found themselves in a foreign land (unwillingly), God was with them and was furthering his plans and purposes through them. Their job was to trust God and be channels of his blessing in those places. Whether they were making their way to the Promised Land, living in the Promised Land, or were exiles in a strange land, God remained their God, they remained his people. His good plans for them stood firm. Unlike the Israelites, Peter's audience was not literally in exile. But just like the Israelites, Peter's audience were called to bring glory to God and blessing to others.

It's probably fair to say that these early Christians faced greater marginalisation than Christians these days in the West. Nevertheless, we too may feel like 'foreigners and exiles' in our nation, at work, or in our communities. At the same time, many Christians are a source of great blessing in their context and God has opened many doors for them to minister grace and love, to be messengers of the gospel. Yes, the media report on Christians taken to court over taking a stand for their faith. Others are sidelined. Yet we have enormous freedom to stand up for our faith. And many Christians have found ways to offer prayer, do good, and build meaningful friendships in their public spaces as well as their personal ones.

Whatever our lot, the call to us as resident aliens is the same: 'be holy in all you do' (1:15), commit yourselves to our 'faithful Creator and continue to do good' (4:19), and in so doing bring glory to God (2:12).

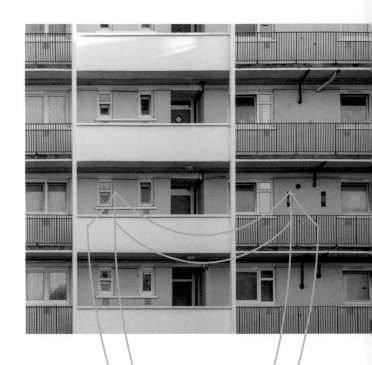

Session 2

Confident in Identity

1 Peter 2:4–10

First Thoughts

Lanyards – everyone seems to wear one these days. I noticed a social worker wearing one when she'd popped into my local store to take advantage of the Meal Deal (which are excellent value in my opinion, especially if you include a smoothie that normally costs £2 on its own).

The lanyard usually bears an ID card. It tells everyone who the wearer is: name, job title, and who they represent. But it also communicates something of the wearer's purpose. During the working day, wherever she is, whatever she's doing, the lanyard remains around the social worker's neck. I imagine that there are situations she goes into where she wonders 'what on earth am I going to do here?' Then she glances down at her ID card and is reminded who she is, and what she's there to do: social work – foster human flourishing.

As the people of God, we too have an identity and a purpose which we carry with us at all times and in all places. Our letter-writer, Peter, considered these foundational for confident living in a complex world. This session explores how Peter helped those early Christians discover the riches of their new identity and how it could radically change their perspective on the challenges they faced.

Read – 1 Peter 2:4-10

⁴ As you come to him, the living Stone – rejected by humans but chosen by God and precious to him – ⁵ you also, like living stones, are being built into a spiritual house to be a holy priesthood, offering spiritual sacrifices acceptable to God through Jesus Christ. ⁶ For in Scripture it says: 'See, I lay a stone in Zion, a chosen and precious cornerstone, and the one who trusts in him will never be put to shame.' ⁷ Now to you who believe, this stone is precious. But to those who do not believe, 'The stone the builders rejected has become the cornerstone,' ⁸ and, 'A stone that causes people to stumble and a rock that makes them fall.' They stumble because they disobey the message – which is also what they were destined for. ⁹ But you are a chosen people, a royal priesthood, a holy nation, God's special possession, that you may declare the praises of him who called you out of darkness into his wonderful light. ¹⁰ Once you were not a people, but now you are the people of God; once you had not received mercy, but now you have received mercy.

Focus on the Theme

1. Think about a role you fulfil outside of church activities during a typical week, for example, looking after kids, work, volunteering, running your home. If you were designing an ID card for that role, what would it say for 'location', 'job title', and 'purpose'?

Name:

Job Title:

Location:

Purpose:

What Does the Bible Say?

2. In 2:4–10, Peter describes the Christians he's writing to in several different ways. Either as a whole group or in pairs, identify the different descriptions he uses. What aspect of their Christian identity was Peter wanting to help them grasp with each one?

Description	Meaning
e.g. Living stones (2:5)	They become part of the 'spiritual house', built around Jesus. Each one of us has a role to play as God's Spirit lives amongst us.

3. Their identity was based on Jesus and what he had done for them. How does Peter encourage them to keep trusting Jesus in 2:4-6?

4. Take a look at Exodus 19:5-6.
What phrases or ideas has Peter borrowed from Exodus and applied to the Christians he is writing to?

Why might he have done this?

5. The first readers of Peter's letters were living in the Roman Empire. What challenges might they have faced in maintaining their Christian identity described in 2:9-10?

Early Christianity in the Roman Empire

The Roman Empire was huge, spanning significant chunks of Asia, Europe, and Africa. There was enormous diversity within it: groups of people with differing customs, cultures, and gods. This created an ongoing challenge for the rulers of the Empire: maintaining peace and social cohesion. Generally speaking, emperors maintained a policy of religious tolerance, allowing local people to continue worshipping their local gods. Back then, most people believed that if you didn't worship the local deities, they might become angry and ruin your harvest, or send a nasty plague, or kill you – so allowing people to continue their regular worship was a smart move, politically speaking.

In addition to worshipping their local gods, subjects of the Empire were required to pay homage to Caesar by declaring that he was 'Lord'. Going above and beyond in emperor worship increased a city's likelihood of receiving financial or political favours. Failing to do so, however, would bring the wrong kind of attention.

Going Deeper 🔍

6. Exodus not only speaks of what God saved his people from (slavery in Egypt), it also speaks of what God saved his people for (to be a people who would know him and make him known). But what does God say about their identity and purpose when they were in exile, in Jeremiah 29:4–14?

What does this show us about the identity and purpose of God's people, wherever they are and whatever the circumstances?

7. Why do you think Peter focuses on their identity so early on in the letter?

Why not just focus on telling them to live good lives?

Living it Out

8. Which aspects of your identity as God's 'chosen people, a royal priesthood, a holy nation, God's special possession' are a particular encouragement at the moment? Why is that?

9. Like Peter's first readers, there are probably people on your frontline who don't believe in Jesus or think he's particularly special. In what way might the truths that Peter has dwelt on help you be more confident as a Christian on your frontline?

10. What's your takeaway from the discussion – a truth to celebrate, a fresh insight to embrace, a distorted perspective to repent of, a commitment to offer, an action to take?

My takeaway:

_____

_____

_____

_____

_____

_____

_____

Prayer Time ♛

- Take a few moments just to reflect again on how you have been affirmed in your identity and purpose through the discussion. Thank God for what has encouraged you.

- In pairs or as a group, share one implication of your discussion for your frontline, and pray for each other.

My frontline implication:

Terms

Spiritual house (2:5)
Israel longed for a renewed, more glorious temple.
The community of Jesus-followers (made up of Jews and Gentiles) has become the place where God's glory and presence dwells.

Chosen people (2:9)
Even though they were predominantly Gentiles, through their relationship with Jesus they have become part of God's people, part of Israel's story, fully wrapped up into God's rich purposes for the world.

Royal priesthood and holy nation (2:9)
All of God's people share in the privilege and responsibility of reflecting God's holy character to the wider world and helping bring people into relationship with God.

KIRSTEN'S STORY

The community school playground where Kirsten lurked for 190 afternoons per year was not the one she'd hoped for. Due to a bumper crop of siblings at her first-choice school, her kids ended up here. As she waited for them to burst out of the main door, she felt again like the 'foreigner' or 'stranger' in the crowd.

'Non-religious' was how the vast majority of parents at the school would class themselves, with the most vocalised belief system being atheism. 'People are aware of my beliefs and it challenges them – so I am never part of the "in" crowd, especially as I don't do the playground gossip.' What would it mean for Kirsten to represent Christ and his kingdom in this strange territory over the 1,865 times she would wait here?

It wasn't long before Kirsten noticed that those who were not the parents of the children they were collecting, such as grandparents and nannies, often found themselves on the fringe – friendless. And so, Kirsten made a deliberate effort to befriend and minister God's grace and love to them.

She got to know a nanny from a non-practising Hindu background. As she and Kirsten chatted, it transpired that this nanny's daughter was desperate to have a baby but had endured the heartache of multiple miscarriages. Kirsten was privileged to be invited into this sad and sacred space and was able to walk alongside this heartbroken lady. Knowing that Kirsten was a Christian, the nanny invited Kirsten to pray for her daughter. Kirsten did. Amazingly, with thanks to God, this nanny is now a very happy grandmother.

Kirsten noticed grandparents and nannies often found themselves on the fringe – friendless.

Now, as Kirsten's youngest heads off to secondary school, she looks back on those 1,865 days she spent in a 'foreign land'. As well as the many conversations she had, prayers she prayed, birthday parties attended and so forth, she's also been able to build a bridge between this school community and her church community. Along with others, she has delivered RE lessons to every year group in the school, has seen 25 children attend the church's holiday club, and eight families have been along to Messy Church. She did not choose this place but it's where her Heavenly Father wanted her to be. His plans are always good.

Session 3

Confident in the World

1 Peter 2:11–25

First Thoughts

Being an acrobat is really hard. Trust me, I've never been one. Though I did once see two acrobats doing their conditioning work in the studio at a holiday resort. They were controlled, flexible too, like gibbons. I could only imagine how many hours they had spent training to get into that kind of shape.

That night, we watched, enthralled, as they tumbled, twisted, and turned in ways we gasping spectators never could. To perform like this, they had to be confident in their own ability, as well as the ability of their partner. They also needed to be confident in the work of the engineers who rigged up the trapeze and high ropes. Then they needed one more thing: an arena. Without that, how could we, the audience, be wowed by the wonder of their talent?

So far, we've seen that Christians need to be confident in the gospel and in their identity in Christ. While our 'audience' may not be spellbound in silent wonder, nor erupting with wild applause as we go about our daily lives, we are nonetheless called to live out our identity in life's arena. Just like these early Christians, we are called to live a Jesus-shaped life in full view of our employees and our employers, our colleagues and our customers, our families and our friends. If we all remain in the studio, we can't shape society for the better. We can't reveal Jesus to those he longs to reach.

Read – 1 Peter 2:11-25

¹¹ Dear friends, I urge you, as foreigners and exiles, to abstain from sinful desires, which wage war against your soul. ¹² Live such good lives among the pagans that, though they accuse you of doing wrong, they may see your good deeds and glorify God on the day he visits us. ¹³ Submit yourselves for the Lord's sake to every human authority: whether to the emperor, as the supreme authority, ¹⁴ or to governors, who are sent by him to punish those who do wrong and to commend those who do right. ¹⁵ For it is God's will that by doing good you should silence the ignorant talk of foolish people. ¹⁶ Live as free people, but do not use your freedom as a cover-up for evil; live as God's slaves. ¹⁷ Show proper respect to everyone, love the family of believers, fear God, honour the emperor. ¹⁸ Slaves, in reverent fear of God submit yourselves to your masters, not only to those who are good and considerate, but also to those who are harsh. ¹⁹ For it is commendable if someone bears up under the pain of unjust suffering because they are conscious of God. ²⁰ But how is it to your credit if you receive a beating for doing wrong and endure it? But if you suffer for doing good and you endure it, this is commendable before God. ²¹ To this you were called, because Christ suffered for you, leaving you an example, that you should follow in his steps. ²² 'He committed no sin, and no deceit was found in his mouth.' ²³ When they hurled their insults at him, he did not retaliate; when he suffered, he made no threats. Instead, he entrusted himself to him who judges justly. ²⁴ 'He himself bore our sins' in his body on the cross, so that we might die to sins and live for righteousness; 'by his wounds you have been healed.' ²⁵ For 'you were like sheep going astray,' but now you have returned to the Shepherd and Overseer of your souls.

Focus on the Theme

1. Who do you respect for the positive difference they've made in the world, and why? It might be someone from the past or present, it could be somebody famous or obscure, perhaps someone in your family or a person you work with.

What Does the Bible Say?

2. 2:11-12 are key verses for understanding the whole of 1 Peter and help to make sense of the instructions he gives in 2:13-20. How would you explain his point in your own words?

3. The Roman Empire was powerful. Nevertheless, according to 2:13-20, who was ultimately in charge?

How might knowing this have boosted the confidence of Christians who felt marginalised and under threat?

4. Bearing in mind the new identity these Christian slaves had in Christ (you can read about first-century slavery on page 50), how did Peter's radical instructions to slaves in 2:18-20 provide them with a new way to view their situation and respond?

How might viewing themselves as God's chosen and holy people, and as royal priests, have enabled them to live out Peter's instructions with confidence?

5. In 2:21-25, what does Peter highlight about the purpose of Christ's death?

How does this shed light on the life of a Christian slave?

Slavery

Estimates of the prevalence of slavery in the first-century
Roman Empire vary wildly – the most conservative
being 25% and some suggesting it could have been
as high as 90%. Whatever the exact figure, slaves
accounted for a significant chunk of the population.
The roles they performed and the way they were
treated varied enormously too. They worked as
housekeepers, farm labourers, construction workers,
doctors, teachers, cooks, and estate managers, and
more. Some fared well and many went on to buy their
own freedom. For others, conditions were atrocious:
cramped and squalid living quarters, meagre rations,
barely clothed, sexually exploited, regularly beaten.

Being a slave didn't just affect how you were treated,
your living conditions, or your autonomy - it went even
deeper. Being a slave was an identity, or perhaps
more accurately, a non-identity. Often, they were
regarded as subhuman. The Greek philosopher,
Aristotle, referred to slaves as 'human tools'.

To be a Christian slave was to be a living paradox. In the
eyes of God you were honoured and free; in the eyes of
the world you were dishonoured and trapped. Options
were limited. Without any rights, their best hope was to
keep their heads down and hope one day to purchase
their freedom. Fighting back against an owner would
result in severe punishment, possibly mutilation or even
death. They knew too well what it meant to be stuck
between a rock and a hard place. Addressing them
specifically, Peter wanted these slaves to see themselves
in the light of 2:12 – they could live in a way that would
help those around them see something of God.

Going Deeper

6. Peter urged them to submit themselves 'to every human authority' (2:13). Do you think Peter expected there to be exceptions to this rule?

What did submission to rulers and governors look like for Jesus and the apostles? What didn't it look like?

7. Of all the New Testament writers, Peter draws the clearest link between Jesus' death and the 'Suffering Servant' of Isaiah 53. Take a look at Isaiah 53. What connections do you see with 1 Peter 2:21–25?

Living it Out

8. Putting modesty to one side for a moment, what have you noticed about one another that demonstrates something about 'living a good life', Monday through Sunday?

9. God calls us to model Christ in difficult circumstances. Is there a specific situation you're facing on your frontline where you need wisdom, grace, or courage?

10. How does the earlier part of Peter's letter around the gospel and our identity in Christ encourage you to live confidently through this?

Prayer Time

- Thank God for one another and the difference each person is making in the world.

- Pray for those who have shared specific frontline situations for which they need God's help to confidently live for him in those places.

- You may prefer to prayerfully listen to your favourite version of the song, *Amazing Love (You are my King)*. As you do so, silently reflect on the beauty and grace of Jesus. Ask him to shape your heart and fill you with his Spirit, so that you can become more like him.

The beauty of Christ

In the midst of advising the people of God about the realities of life, Peter gives us a beautiful portrait of Jesus (1 Peter 2:21-25).

Imagine walking into a rather run-down factory and discovering a random set of materials adorning the tired walls. To the left you spot a promotional calendar from a company that manufactures forklift trucks. To the right, a rather drab poster from the Health & Safety Executive. Suddenly you see it. Hanging between these two is the original painting, *The Water-Lily Pond*, by Claude Monet. 'What on earth is that beautiful picture doing here?' you ask yourself. It's a somewhat fantastical scenario. Yet reading 1 Peter 2:13-3:7 has something of that kind of impact.

In 2:13-20, Peter writes about life under government (which everyone knew was corrupt) and how to respond to slave masters (who would sometimes beat up their slaves without reason). Further on in 3:1-7, he confronts the very real challenges women in the Greco-Roman world faced when they trusted in Jesus, and their husbands didn't. And the challenge, too, for Christian husbands to live counter-culturally. This was the stuff of day-to-day life: the messy, the ugly, and the ordinary. It's in the midst of these realities that Peter chooses to hang this beautiful portrait of Jesus (2:21-25). And it really is beautiful.

Christ, the Son of God, the one who had delighted in the Father's presence for all eternity, willingly chose to suffer for us (2:21). Truth and integrity were the fabric of his life and words (2:22). He was without sin. When mocked, spat on, beaten, and nailed naked to a Roman cross, he didn't retaliate (2:23). He bore the full weight of the judgement we deserved, so that we might be made whole, set free for abundant life, our relationship with the Father fully restored (2:24-25). The parallels between this description of Jesus, and the picture painted by Isaiah of the Suffering Servant (Isaiah 53) are not accidental. Peter is clear: Jesus is the long-awaited Christ, and it's through his sacrificial death that we enter God's kingdom (2:24-25).

But the death of Jesus isn't only the way into the Kingdom. It lays down a pattern for life in the Kingdom. We are called to follow the example of Christ (2:21). This isn't a part-time pursuit, reserved for religious days, times, or ceremonies. Hanging the picture where he does, Peter makes a profound point. In the monotonous, difficult, and unfair aspects of life, those bits we might be tempted to write off as the necessary evils of existence – as well as the joyous opportunities of life – he beckons us to follow and love like him. Apprenticed to Christ, we learn the ways of Jesus in our everyday contexts, in a complex world.

Session 4

Confident in Relationships

1 Peter 3:1–12

First Thoughts

You may be familiar with the TV series, Dragons' Den, in which budding entrepreneurs get three minutes to pitch their business idea to five multi-millionaires potentially willing to invest their own cash. Tone and posture matter. Demanding investment is a sure way to the exit. What's needed is confident, yet humble persuasion.

Yee Kwan had developed a range of quality ice creams, including flavours such as black sesame seed, and lychee. Not only were the customary power dynamics in play, but she was selling products quite different from the norm. Early on in her presentation, Yee gave each Dragon three flavours to sample. Apart from one Dragon, they all loved them. However, the ice cream market is difficult to conquer, and three Dragons declined to invest. But Yee's glorious flavours and winsome approach persuaded two to make an offer.

Being a Christian in the Roman Empire during the first century required humility and a willingness to embrace weakness. Like selling weird ice cream flavours, it was a major break from the norm. Peter was by no means expecting every person these Christians had contact with to choose to invest their lives in Jesus, but he knew if they could taste and see, some would.

Read – 1 Peter 3:1–12

[1] Wives, in the same way submit yourselves to your own husbands so that, if any of them do not believe the word, they may be won over without words by the behaviour of their wives, [2] when they see the purity and reverence of your lives. [3] Your beauty should not come from outward adornment, such as elaborate hairstyles and the wearing of gold jewellery or fine clothes. [4] Rather, it should be that of your inner self, the unfading beauty of a gentle and quiet spirit, which is of great worth in God's sight. [5] For this is the way the holy women of the past who put their hope in God used to adorn themselves. They submitted themselves to their own husbands, [6] like Sarah, who obeyed Abraham and called him her lord. You are her daughters if you do what is right and do not give way to fear. [7] Husbands, in the same way be considerate as you live with your wives, and treat them with respect as the weaker partner and as heirs with you of the gracious gift of life, so that nothing will hinder your prayers. [8] Finally, all of you, be like-minded, be sympathetic, love one another, be compassionate and humble. [9] Do not repay evil with evil or insult with insult. On the contrary, repay evil with blessing, because to this you were called so that you may inherit a blessing. [10] For, 'Whoever would love life and see good days must keep their tongue from evil and their lips from deceitful speech. [11] They must turn from evil and do good; they must seek peace and pursue it. [12] For the eyes of the Lord are on the righteous and his ears are attentive to their prayer, but the face of the Lord is against those who do evil.'

Focus on the Theme

1. Can you think of a time when somebody influenced you for the better? Perhaps they encouraged you in a good habit or a positive action. What was it about that person that made you listen to them?

What Does the Bible Say?

2. Given the place of wives in the household in New Testament times, how might those wives who decided to follow Jesus have felt if they had a husband who still worshipped pagan gods? What might they have been tempted to do?

3. Peter starts with the words, 'Wives, in the same way', referring to the example of Christ in 2:21–25. (You can read commentary on 2:21–25 on page 44, and the feature about Christian wives on page 50.) What attitudes and actions did Peter encourage these women to embrace?

4. He repeats the phrase, 'in the same way', in 3:7 when he gives advice to Christian husbands. What attitudes and actions did Peter encourage these men to embrace?

5. How do the virtues that Peter encourages in 3:8–12 foster good relationships?

Going Deeper

6. Drawing on this passage and others that might come to mind, why do you think God chooses to work through people in situations where they lack social power?

What does this say about God?

7. How does having confidence in the gospel (session 1) and in Christian identity (session 2) build confidence when a person is in a position of relational weakness?

Christian wives and household gods

First-century Greek and Roman culture was largely dominated by men. Women tended to be viewed as cognitively inferior and less trustworthy than men. Therefore, they had less access to education, social and political power, and justice. Families, which were seen as integral to a healthy society, generally had clear divisions of power, with the father figure (known as the paterfamilias) being ultimately responsible for, and in charge of, everyone within the household.

The following quote from the Greek thinker and writer, Plutarch (AD 46-120), provides an interesting backdrop to Peter's instructions: 'A woman ought not to make friends of her own, but to enjoy her husband's friends in common with him. The gods are the first and foremost important friends. Hence, it is becoming for a wife to worship and to know only the gods that her husband believes in, and to shut the door tight upon all strange rituals and outlandish superstitions.'

The situation on the ground likely varied from place to place and family to family, as it does in our own time. While Christian wives of non-Christian husbands may have been limited in their options, Peter's advice is practical, encouraging them to live in a way which is shaped by the pattern of Christ and motivated by missional concerns. Reflecting his instructions to all Christians to 'live such good lives among the pagans' (2:12), wives are an integral part of the witness of the church as a whole. Now as then, those in marriages where the other partner is not a believer need the love and support of the church community and wisdom about how best to live as a Christian in their home context.

Living it Out

8. Why do you think some people who aren't Christians struggle when those close to them become Christians?

Have you experienced this in your family, friendships, or at work?

9. Is there a particular relationship on your frontline that is difficult?

How does this passage help you think or pray about it?

10. In what ways does Peter's invitation to live like Christ in your relationships challenge or encourage you?

Prayer Time

• Thank God that he is able to work through you to point others to himself, whatever your relationship with those people might be.

• Share one 'virtue' that you'd like to grow in that will strengthen your relationships.

• Pray for someone close to you who doesn't know Christ. Ask God to give you wisdom and courage to live like him. Pray that they will be 'won over'.

ADAM'S STORY

Most days, Adam's frontline is a workshop. On this particular day, it was clear that his colleague Terry was angry. A steel pole hits the concrete floor. Clang! Followed by a hammer. It was only the two of them in the workshop that day and, under normal circumstances, Adam could have talked Tempestuous Terry down. But this day was not a normal day.

In the weeks leading up to this day, Terry had barely spoken to Adam. The reason for this was Terry had left Adam stranded at a site where they'd been working, meaning Adam got home really late that night. Perhaps unwisely, Adam had sent a sarcastic text, but he was genuinely willing to put the whole thing behind them. Terry was having none of it. What had been a healthy friendship, where Adam had had some great conversations with Terry about Jesus, became a fractured working relationship. Terry would only talk to Adam about work, and only when he had to.

Back to that day in the workshop. Tools and metalwork continued to crash, and Adam prayed. He longed to be a blessing in Terry's life, to be a good friend to him. 'Father, please provide a way for this relationship to be restored.' Within seconds, Adam received the quickest answer to prayer he'd ever experienced... and it came in the shape of a 4 ½ inch aluminium oxide grinding disc. Unaware of Adam's precise location, Terry had flung this CD-sized disc across the room. But instead of smashing into a wall or machine, it hit Adam straight on the head, resulting instantly in a deep gash. As the blood poured from Adam's temple, Terry rushed over in a state of shock and remorse. 'Are you OK? I'm so sorry! I really didn't mean for that to happen!'

Adam's colleague wouldn't even talk to him.

How would Adam respond?

Not in (justified) anger, not in (understandable) retaliation, but with (remarkable) love, Adam reassured Terry that he was fine, that he wasn't angry, and that it was OK. In that instant, all the tension between these workmates dissipated, and within minutes they were both laughing. Neither of them needed to say anything about the previous fall out and the sarcastic text. Conversations about films, family, and faith resumed. A few months down the line, Terry faced a significant health problem. In all the challenges that he and his family faced, Adam was there to walk with them, offering practical support, comfort, and prayer.

Discovering Old Testament riches through the New

Although the Bible comes to us in two parts – the Old Testament (OT) and the New Testament (NT) – they belong together, with the NT understood as a continuation and fulfilment of the OT. That is why the NT frequently alludes to the OT and often quotes it directly.

We saw this continuation in session 2, where, in 1 Peter 2:4-10, Peter makes it clear that the church is not a brand-new project disconnected from God's OT people. Rather, by applying the language of Exodus 19:5-6, Peter helps Christians to see they are being written into the story God has been working on for a long time. In Exodus, God powerfully saves his people, then shows them how to live in a way that would bring blessing to themselves and the entire world. It's in this context he refers them as a 'kingdom of priests and a holy nation'. By applying this language to Christians who have also experienced God's salvation, Peter makes plain they are now part of God's one people, his one family. We are part of this people who are blessed, and who in turn bless the world and point others to God.

Sometimes the writers of the NT letters reference the OT to show how it predicted what Jesus would be like, and what he would do. We see this in 1 Peter 2:22, where Peter quotes Isaiah 53:9. Isaiah foresaw God's suffering servant would be sinless in every way. The integrity of his words would reveal this. Peter points back to this, saying: look at Jesus, even when he was being mocked and crucified, he did not sin or retaliate in actions or with words. He is the one Isaiah said would come.

The use of the OT in the NT is not limited to predictions though. Sometimes, the OT is used to demonstrate how Jesus, or life in his Kingdom, aligns with the way God worked within the OT. For instance, Peter quotes Proverbs 3:34 in 1 Peter 5:5: 'God opposes the proud but gives grace to the humble.' He does this to encourage Christians to trust God through difficult circumstances. He does not change; he is faithful and true to his word. So, he will strengthen them. That's how he worked back then, and he continues to work like that now.

At other times, NT writers, such as Peter, refer to characters, events, or rituals from the OT. They then show how Jesus and the Kingdom he brings are somehow like that character/event/ritual, only better. An example of this is 1 Peter 2:7, which references Psalm 118. In this Psalm, a king was in a military situation where the odds were stacked against him (Psalm 118:10 says 'all the nations surrounded' him). Yet because his trust was in God, he was victorious. It didn't matter that people doubted his abilities; the fact is, he won. The reason Peter refers to this king is to say something profound about Jesus. Most people didn't recognise Jesus as a conquering king who could bring salvation. Yet, just like the king in Psalm 118, Jesus is a 'stone the builders rejected' (2:7) who turns out to be the most important stone in the building project. Jesus didn't just bring a temporary or local military victory, but permanent and global salvation.

The OT also contains characters the NT writers hold up as examples, whether good or bad. Here, Peter points back to Sarah, the wife of Abraham, noting the inner beauty of her character (3:4).

Session 5

Confident in Witness

1 Peter 3:13–4:6

First Thoughts

They pop up online all the time nowadays – customer service chat boxes. Whether you're researching a new bike, working out how to invest your pennies, or choosing a hotel in Tenerife (or Tenby), you've probably had one of those little boxes pop up offering you a 'chat' with a member of staff. Proactive companies know potential customers often have questions. They know they may not discover these answers all by themselves. Or, worse still, they'll discover the answers on a competitor's website! Good customer service agents do their best to understand what it is you want to know, then provide you with the relevant information in a clear and easy to understand way. When the agent has answered your question(s), they may ask if there is anything else they can help you with, and they may suggest some next steps. The best of them do all this in a personable and non-pushy way. Of course, this session isn't about engaging with 'potential customers' in the hope they'll 'buy our products or services'. But it is about how we can respond well when those on our frontlines ask us questions about our faith in Jesus.

Read – 1 Peter 3:13-18 & 4:1-6

3:13 Who is going to harm you if you are eager to do good? 14 But even if you should suffer for what is right, you are blessed. 'Do not fear their threats; do not be frightened.' 15 But in your hearts revere Christ as Lord. Always be prepared to give an answer to everyone who asks you to give the reason for the hope that you have. But do this with gentleness and respect, 16 keeping a clear conscience, so that those who speak maliciously against your good behaviour in Christ may be ashamed of their slander. 17 For it is better, if it is God's will, to suffer for doing good than for doing evil. 18 For Christ also suffered once for sins, the righteous for the unrighteous, to bring you to God. He was put to death in the body but made alive in the Spirit.

4:1 Therefore, since Christ suffered in his body, arm yourselves also with the same attitude, because whoever suffers in the body has finished with sin. 2 As a result, they do not live the rest of their earthly lives for evil human desires, but rather for the will of God. 3 For you have spent enough time in the past doing what pagans choose to do – living in debauchery, lust, drunkenness, orgies, carousing and detestable idolatry. 4 They are surprised that you do not join them in their reckless, wild living, and they heap abuse on you. 5 But they will have to give account to him who is ready to judge the living and the dead. 6 For this is the reason the gospel was preached even to those who are now dead, so that they might be judged according to human standards in regard to the body but live according to God in regard to the spirit.

Focus on the Theme

1. Can you think of a time someone on your frontline made a comment about or asked about your Christian faith? What did they say? How did the conversation go?

What Does the Bible Say?

2. Before he writes about answering questions, Peter first encourages these Christians not to be frightened (3:14). Why does Peter assume fear might be an issue for them?

3. Peter says they should be prepared to give the 'reason for the hope' that they have (3:15). What reasons for hope do you think Peter has in mind?

4. In 3:15-16, Peter makes it clear it isn't just about what his readers say, but the way they say it. In what manner should they talk about their faith?

Why would this form an important part of their witness?

5. What challenges were these Christians facing (4:1-6)?

In what way is living a Christ-like life a witness too?

Going Deeper

6. In 4:4-5, Peter refers to God's future judgement, and how it should shape how people live in the present. What else does Peter have to say about how the future should shape how we live now?

You may find it helpful to break into pairs, with each pair looking at one or two of the following verses: 1:3-9; 1:13; 2:12; 4:7; 4:12-19; 5:1-6; and 5:10-11.

7. Look at 1 Peter 3:19-22 in your Bible. Why do you think Peter included these verses?

Living it Out

8. In what way would you like to grow in confidence in your Christian witness?

9. Pause to pray and ask God to remind each person in the group of a person who isn't a Christian, someone he'd like you to pray for, love, and be a witness to.

In pairs, give a pen portrait of that person – their character, situation, what they think about Christian faith, about Jesus. What do you think a good next step in their faith journey might be?

10. If you had the opportunity to 'give a reason for the hope that you have' to that person, what kind of things would you say?

Prayer Time

Pray for the people you've talked about, asking God that he will give you the opportunity to be a good witness to them and to speak well of Christ.

EMILY'S STORY

Holes in the wall, stains on the carpets, and mouldy plates piled up next to the sink. People were constantly in and out. If you wanted to sleep, you somehow had to drift off with drum and bass music pounding through the wall. Casual sex, excessive drinking, and recreational drug use were the norm in these halls of residence. During her first year at university, this is where Emily called home.

She was confident though. Confident in the truth and power of the gospel, confident of her identity in Christ, and confident that God could work through her in this place. Though she may not have used this language to describe herself, she saw herself as one of God's 'royal priests'; her life could point others to Jesus.

Living well in this grotty context meant not doing some things. Sleeping around, illicit drugs, and heavy drinking were most definitely off the menu! But living out her identity and purpose meant more than saying 'no' to certain things, it meant saying 'yes' to other things. 'Yes' to caring for friends, 'yes' to having fun, 'yes' to blessing others, 'yes' to sharing Jesus. On a few occasions, people accused Emily of being boring, a killjoy. But in the face of Emily's kind and joyous life, their words rang hollow. Everyone knew Emily made their lives better.

On a few occasions,
people accused Emily of
being boring, a killjoy.

Anna was one such person. A 'work hard, party hard'
kind of girl, Anna had never given serious thought to
Christian faith. As far as she was concerned, all religions
were basically the same... and she needed none of them.
Yet there was something about the life Emily lived, and
the Jesus she talked about that Anna couldn't dismiss.
She'd ask Emily questions, read things Emily gave her, ask
more questions. Emily bought Anna a Bible, which she
began to read, and she would sometimes go to church
with Emily too. Just before Christmas in their second
year, Emily sensed it was the moment to invite Anna to
follow Jesus. By the end of the holidays, via a visit to a
local church, Anna had surrendered to Jesus' love. When
she came back the following term, everyone could see
something significant had changed in her life, and it was
eventually through Anna that another girl from their house
became a Christian. But that's a story for another time.

What shall we make of suffering?

The Bible has a lot to say about suffering, not only suffering as a consequence of persecution. In this letter, however, Peter focuses on the kind of suffering Christians can experience as a result of pledging allegiance to Jesus when they live among people who reject him. As we read through the letter, it helps to bear this in mind as we consider how this might help us today.

Having said that, much of what he says to encourage Christians suffering in that specific way can strengthen and encourage us as we suffer in other ways too. In 1 Peter, then, we might learn from:

The pervasiveness of suffering amongst Christians
Christians in that time and region experienced 'all kinds of trials' (1:6), such as false and malicious accusations (2:12; 3:16), physical beatings from slave masters (2:18-20), relational pressure (3:1-6) and insults (3:9; 4:4). It's clear these were not exceptional cases. As we know, Peter's audience was spread across a wide area and he recognises that 'Christians throughout the world' were suffering a similar backlash (5:9). Christians aren't immune from suffering.

The pain they were experiencing
Though Peter puts their suffering into perspective, enables them to see its purpose, and calls them to persevere, at no time does he minimise the pain they were experiencing. In the same breath as declaring that they rejoice, he also clarifies that they 'suffer grief' (1:6), that they are suffering a 'painful trial' (4:12). These were real people who were not impervious to physical, emotional, or social pain.

The purpose they saw in suffering
Yes, the suffering was real and yes, it was painful, but it wasn't pointless. Christians suffered unfairly at the hands of masters, neighbours, business associates, and even their own family members. As these Christians responded with grace, they pointed people to God (2:12), demonstrating the reality of Christ, and perhaps provoking questions about 'the hope' they possessed (3:15). Not only could suffering lead to good witness to Christ but it could also purify their faith and prove its genuineness (1:6-7).

The perspective they cultivated

As followers of a crucified Lord, who suffered in all kinds of ways (2:21-24; 4:1), Peter reassures them that suffering shouldn't be a surprise (4:12). Following Christ in a pagan culture would inevitably mean suffering, but that suffering would not be permanent. They might suffer for 'a little while' (1:6; 5:10) but 'The end of all things is near' (4:7). God will judge (4:5-6), and a time is coming when Christ's glory will be revealed (4:13). Peter assured them that God himself would restore them and make them 'strong, firm, and steadfast' (5:10).

The perseverance they developed

The possibility of fear, misery, retaliation, and abandoning the faith were all too real for Christians back then, as they are for any who suffer. Don't go down these dead ends, Peter implored them. Do not repay evil for evil (3:9). Rejoice (4:13)! 'Do not be frightened' (3:13), rather 'set apart Christ as Lord' and 'be prepared to give an answer to everyone who asks you to give the reason for the hope that you have' (3:15). Resist the devil and stand firm in the faith (5:9).

Session 6

Confident in Community

1 Peter 4:7–5:14

First Thoughts

Being a professional boxer, there's a tough job. For three whole minutes, it's just you and your opponent, and nobody can help you. And, unless one of you gets KO'd or the fight gets stopped, you have to do those three minutes up to twelve times. Sticking to the game plan is one of the hardest things. As Mike Tyson famously said: 'Everyone has a plan until they get punched in the mouth.' The good news for boxers is that in between each three-minute round, they can return to their corner. Here, their team can refresh them and patch up their cuts. They give them feedback on the round that just went, advice for the round ahead and, perhaps most importantly, encouragement. As Christians step out into the world each week, they expend energy, they are focused on fighting the good fight, and they may take a few hits too. Then the bell rings, the church community gathers together to be refreshed, patched up, reminded of the game plan, and encouraged to keep going.

Read – 1 Peter 4:7-11 and 5:1-11

---

⁴:⁷ The end of all things is near. Therefore, be alert and of sober mind so that you may pray. ⁸ Above all, love each other deeply, because love covers over a multitude of sins. ⁹ Offer hospitality to one another without grumbling. ¹⁰ Each of you should use whatever gift you have received to serve others, as faithful stewards of God's grace in its various forms. ¹¹ If anyone speaks, they should do so as one who speaks the very words of God. If anyone serves, they should do so with the strength God provides, so that in all things God may be praised through Jesus Christ. To him be the glory and the power for ever and ever. Amen.

⁵:¹ To the elders among you, I appeal as a fellow elder and a witness of Christ's sufferings who also will share in the glory to be revealed: ² be shepherds of God's flock that is under your care, watching over them – not because you must, but because you are willing, as God wants you to be; not pursuing dishonest gain, but eager to serve; ³ not lording it over those entrusted to you, but being examples to the flock. ⁴ And when the Chief Shepherd appears, you will receive the crown of glory that will never fade away. ⁵ In the same way, you who are younger, submit yourselves to your elders. All of you, clothe yourselves with humility towards one another, because, 'God opposes the proud but shows favour to the humble.' ⁶ Humble yourselves, therefore, under God's mighty hand, that he may lift you up in due time. ⁷ Cast all your anxiety on him because he cares for you. ⁸ Be alert and of sober mind. Your enemy the devil prowls around like a roaring lion looking for someone to devour. ⁹ Resist him, standing firm in the faith, because you know that the family of believers throughout the world is undergoing the same kind of sufferings. ¹⁰ And the God of all grace, who called you to his eternal glory in Christ, after you have suffered a little while, will himself restore you and make you strong, firm and steadfast. ¹¹ To him be the power for ever and ever. Amen.

Focus on the Theme ⊕

1. Think of a skill that you have, e.g. playing an instrument, a sport, cooking, etc. Who helped you develop this ability, and how? Think of those who helped you directly (e.g. a coach or teacher) and indirectly (e.g. a book author or YouTube creator).

What Does the Bible Say? 🔖

2. Skim the section between the passages here, 1 Peter 4:12-19, in your Bible. What challenges were these Christians facing?

3. In light of these, what actions and values does Peter call Christians to embrace in 4:8-11?

In what sense could the Christian community act as a 'boxer's corner'?

4. As you look at 4:7-11 and 5:1-5, how is God involved in the way Christians relate to one another?

5. In what way do 5:6-11 add to the picture of Christian community that Peter has painted?

Going Deeper

6. The society these Christians were living in had a strict hierarchy. The 'important' people expected to be served and honoured by those 'below' them in the social pecking order. In what ways was this hierarchy broken down within the church?

7. Thinking about the letter as a whole, how does Peter draw on the big story the Bible tells to encourage these Christians to stand firm in their faith in a complex world?

Living it Out

8. How does being a community of disciples help you be confident in your Monday to Saturday life?

Has this study suggested ways you could grow in this?

9. Take a look at some of the challenges and opportunities you noted at the beginning of this study series. In what ways have you seen God at work?

10. What's the 'one thing' that you want to take away from this study on 1 Peter?

The author's main message

' 12 With the help of Silas, whom I regard as a faithful brother, I have written to you briefly, encouraging you and testifying that this is the true grace of God. Stand fast in it.'

Often ancient letters were dictated by the author to a scribe (or amanuensis). To confirm it really was a letter from them, authors sometimes wrote a personal note at the end with their own hand. This personal note often revealed what was really on the author's mind. In signing off his letter, Peter states his primary purpose in writing: 'encouraging you and testifying that this is the true grace of God. Stand fast in it' (5:12). Despite what they were going through, Peter did not expect his audience to limp to the finish line, but to stand strong, to be confident in the gospel.

Prayer Time

- Give thanks to God for whatever ways he has encouraged, taught, or challenged you through the study.

- Pray for the 'one thing' for one another.

- Close by praying these words together:

  We are a chosen people,
  a royal priesthood,
  a holy nation,
  a people belonging to God,
  not because of anything we
  have done, but because of God's
  grace to us in Christ Jesus.

  By the power of the Holy Spirit,
  let us live our whole lives in a way
  that points others to Jesus,
  for the glory of God.

  Amen.

Epilogue

At the end of this study of
1 Peter, try to find a time when
you can review the whole
study prayerfully before God.

What was the most significant
insight for you from the book?

_____

_____

_____

What did you learn about
reading biblical letters?

_____

_____

_____

Looking back on what was
happening on your frontline
when you started, how have
you seen God at work?

_____

_____

_____

Further reading on 1 Peter

The following list offers some further reading on 1 Peter for those who might like to dig deeper into the letter.

Everyday Church: Mission by Being Good Neighbours

Tim Chester & Steve Timmis

Nottingham: IVP, 2011

1 Peter, The Two Horizons New Testament Commentary

Joel B. Green

Grand Rapids: Eerdmans, 2007

Outposts of Hope: First Peter's Christ for Culture Strategy

Douglas D. Webster

Eugene: Cascade Books, 2015

Other resources from LICC

The One About...
———

Eight stories about God in our everyday

There is no such thing as an ordinary day for a Christian. With Christ, every day, every task, every relationship brims with divine possibility. God is always at work in our lives. But can we see it?

Suitable for individual reading or group reflection, this inspiring collection of true stories told by Mark Greene, Executive Director of LICC, offers us a window into the rich, varied, and sometimes surprising ways God works in our everyday lives.

licc.org.uk/theoneabout

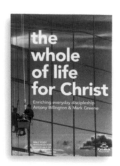

The Whole of Life for Christ

Seven Bible Studies for Individuals and Small Groups

Suppose for a moment that Jesus really is interested in every aspect of your life. This isn't just a nice idea - it's threaded right through the Bible. The deeper we dig into God's word the more we're affirmed in our calling to be disciples of Jesus in every area of our lives.

These seven studies, developed by Antony Billington and Mark Greene in partnership with Keswick Ministries, also include leader's material to inform and prompt group discussion.

licc.org.uk/wlfc

LICC Website

Whether you're looking to grow in your understanding of the Bible and its implications for your daily life, understand how to respond to the pressures and opportunities in today's world or workplace, or looking for resources to help you as you lead a whole-life disciplemaking community, LICC's website is packed full of articles, videos, stories, and resources to help you on your journey. Sign up for weekly Bible reflections, blog posts, prayer journeys and more.

licc.org.uk

About LICC

What difference does following Jesus make to our ordinary Monday to Saturday lives out in God's world? And how can we bring his wisdom, hope, grace, and truth to the things we do every day, to the people we're usually with, and the places we naturally spend time?

Vital questions in any era. After all, the 98% of UK Christians who aren't in church-paid work spend 95% of their time away from church, much of it with the 94% of our fellow-citizens who don't know Jesus. Tragically, most Christians in the UK don't feel equipped to make the most of those opportunities. But what if they were?

That's what we at LICC are seeking to achieve. We work with individuals, church leaders, and theological educators from across the denominations. We delve into the Bible, think hard about the culture we're in, listen carefully to God's people, explore their challenges and opportunities... And we pray, write, speak, train, consult, research, develop, and test resources that offer the biblical frameworks, the lived examples, the practical skills, and the spiritual practices that enable God's people to know him more richly in their everyday lives, and grow as fruitful, whole-life followers of Christ right where they are, on their everyday frontlines, to the glory of God, and the blessing and salvation of many.

To find out more, including ways you can receive news of our latest resources, events, and articles, by email or post, go to **licc.org.uk**

The London Institute for Contemporary Christianity